HOLY UNREST

KYLE & CASSIE RANEY

HOPE COLLLECTIVE PUBLISHING

HOLY UNREST

Published in the United States by Hope Collective Publishing, 2023.

Softcover: ISBN 9798869744159

TO OUR TEAM...

When God first set our feet on the path of
marketplace ministry within the Social Selling
industry, He graced us not only with a calling but
also with a family to share in this purpose. You,
our cherished team, are the joy in our hearts and
the driving force behind this meaningful journey.
Your presence has not only brought hope into our
lives but has extended that hope to countless
others. With deep gratitude, we thank you for
your Kingdom partnership.

CONTENTS

Sometimes our definition of ministry is too small.

INTRODUCTION

*Y*ou are precisely where you need to be.

That still small whisper was our anchor when God shifted us from pastoral ministry to full-time Social Selling. For over fifteen years, all we knew was a life of serving within our local church, and we never imagined we would do anything else.

Stepping away from church ministry into the realm of network marketing felt unconventional, and there were moments when we questioned if we might have misunderstood the Lord's guidance. However, God made it abundantly clear that He was not calling us out of ministry but simply changing where that ministry would take place.

We traded the pulpit for the marketplace, and our small groups transformed into team meetings. Our mission field expanded far beyond the church walls, connecting us with people worldwide and allowing the gospel to go forth by means of which we could have never fathomed.

We have discovered a new depth to our ministry, realizing that every interaction, every meeting, is an opportunity to spread love, grace, and the transformative message of Jesus. While the marketplace wasn't our initial mission field, it has proven to be a fruitful arena to build the Kingdom.

Not long after God led us into Social Selling, He made it clear that our pastoral background would be used for the future equipping of fellow Christians serving this industry. This devotional stands as a tangible marker of that calling.

At its core, this journey together will explore the concept of the "holy unrest," that sacred stirring of the soul that ignites a passion for working diligently in the service of others and for the glory of God.

As followers of Christ in Social Selling, we have been called to something greater than achieving a rank, earning incentives, or creating wealth. Our passion for products and services pales in comparison to our desire to make Jesus known.

For the next 30 days, we will explore our holy *identity*, holy *calling*, holy *actions*, and holy *trust* through Scripture. We believe God will challenge and encourage you to build a business that will impact others for eternity.

God is crafting a movement of His redemptive story within this industry. You are precisely where you need to be, and we believe God will do incredible things IN and THROUGH your YES to Him.

Let the journey begin.

"ambassadors for Christ"
define ambassador:

HOLY IDENTITY

1

RESTLESS PEACE

"Whatever you do, work heartily, as for the Lord and not for men."
Colossians 3:23 ESV

Peace. There may not be another word that can capture such a range of emotions as the word 'peace.' It is what our souls long for and hope to experience as we pursue our purpose each day. Peace is the <u>calm</u> one experiences when you are <u>in God's will</u> and the <u>confidence</u> that pours over us when we answer His call.

We often conceive of peace as those serene moments when chaos is absent, and we find refuge from the problems surrounding us. Yet, <u>true peace</u> is more than a mere absence of turmoil; it is an <u>unwavering assurance</u>. It is the confidence that, <u>regardless of the trials we encounter, God not only accompanies us but will steadfastly remain by our side</u>, <u>never abandoning us no matter where our journey leads.</u>

After 15 years of serving the church through pastoral ministry, God called us to a new platform of service, building a business in the Social Selling industry. This was not in our plans when we first took up the calling from God to impact other people with the good news of Jesus, but almost a decade later, this has proven to be one of the most significant platforms to expand the Kingdom we have ever known.

You may know it as Network Marketing or Direct Sales, but regardless of the term you prefer, one thing is certain: this industry attracts millions of people yearly. Many of whom are followers of Jesus who desire to serve others. Through countless conversations we notice that most simply want to find peace in their business. They seek a template from Scripture that will direct them in their entrepreneurship. They desire an assurance from the Lord that they are right in the center of His will.

If you feel a similar stirring as a Social Seller, know that the peace you seek between your business and your faith is possible. God wants to pour out His peace because He has grand plans to use your passion to serve others, provide for your loved ones, and glorify His name in the process. ♡

We know that doubt, fear, and struggle are a part of this journey. As a Christian, one often wrestles with building a business in an industry that promotes recognition, ambition, and goals. But we are here to encourage you that your business can be purpose-filled when aligned with God. Be at peace, friend. Scripture reveals that we can be motivated and driven to achieve goals (yes, even financial ones) while still having the mission of God be the fuel that propels us forward.

In Colossians 3:23, Paul proclaims that our motivation should always center around the Lord, no matter what we do in this life. This includes our business within Social Selling. We work "heartily" for God and not for the approval of man.

When we do this we can have peace.

As we personally navigated how to infuse our faith within our Social Selling business, we developed a term called "holy unrest." When you have peace in your relationship with Christ while at the same time sensing a restlessness in your spirit to pursue goals that God has laid before you, my friend, you are in a state of holy unrest. For the next 30 days, we will unpack how to harness this holy unrest to find peace in your business and a purposed platform for God's redemptive message.

When our mindset, actions, and motivations align with God's mission, we do not need to fear being out of sync with God's will. The holy unrest within our souls is not meant to be tamed.

When you work within a holy unrest mindset, remember you are doing so for the Lord and not for the acknowledgment of others. You are motivated because Christ has redeemed you, and now you can run freely towards your goals. May the peace that can only be found through Christ permeate your business as you bring good to others and glory to God.

Purpose
Passion
Peace
Prayer
Platform

> ❝
>
> *When our mindset, actions, and motivations are in alignment with God's mission, then we do not need to fear that we are out of sync with God's will.*

COLOSSIANS
3:17

AND WHATEVER YOU DO,
IN WORD OR DEED,
DO EVERYTHING IN THE
NAME OF THE LORD
JESUS, GIVING THANKS TO
GOD THE FATHER
THROUGH HIM.

2

MISTAKEN IDENTITY

> *"Therefore, if anyone is in Christ, he is a new creation.*
> *The old has passed away; behold, the new has come."*
> *2nd Corinthians 5:17 ESV*

It is challenging to discern God's calling when our confidence in who we are in Christ is uncertain. An identity crisis leads to searching for our worth through things outside our relationship with Christ, which will always leave us unfulfilled.

Think for a second about how, when meeting someone for the first time, the question most commonly asked is what they do for a living. We live in a world that links identity to the sum of our activity. A culture that has convinced us that the value of who we are depends solely on our success. However, God does not work in that type of economy. We know that titles fade, and recognition is never constant, but who we are in Christ never waivers.

While there is nothing wrong with finding joy or satisfaction in your victories, we must fight the temptation that those wins shape our identity because success is fleeting and always leaves us feeling incomplete. We were not meant to be identified by our success or achievements alone but by the works of Christ on our behalf. Who we are in Jesus will stand the test of time, and the value of that identity is immeasurable.

5

♡ Amen. And what does He want me to do?

2 Corinthians 5:17 states that we are "new creations" in Christ. Not just part of us is made new, but the entirety of who we are is fully transformed. That means our identity and how we define ourselves changed as well.

Our earthly motivations are buried with Jesus, and we are raised as redeemed souls. We no longer have a drive to serve our own ambitions but are compelled to serve Jesus. We still live in this broken world, but we no longer live for what the world has to offer. Instead, we desire to be recognized as one who belongs to Christ.

New creations have new identities. Our "old creation" has passed away. It no longer remains, nor do the characteristics that defined us before meeting Jesus. If Christ is our primary identifier in this new creation life, then any achievement we earn can complement that identity, but it should never replace it.

Within business, your points, paychecks, titles, and earnings may change, but your identity remains firmly rooted in Christ. We are known by a God who is there to celebrate in the mountain-top moments but also carries us in the valley seasons.

We know that all we ever accomplish in this life is a gift from the Lord. These gifts are an opportunity to celebrate His goodness and give all the glory to God. Upon encountering Jesus, we, as new creations, awaken to a transformed life. Our former selves dissolve, unveiling the wonder of the person God is intricately crafting us to become.

Titus 3:5 tells us that our salvation is founded in God's mercy and the renewal of the Holy Spirit. There are not enough works to perform to earn the type of favor or build that identity that we gain through faith in Christ. When we are resolved that our identity in Jesus is firmly established, the pressure to create an identity from our works fades.

♥ Embracing our new identity in Jesus, deeply rooted in Him, liberates us to pursue achievements without being defined by them. Despite the fluctuations in business sales, there is peace in the unwavering understanding that our identity in Jesus stands firm.

You are who Christ has redeemed you to be, and nothing you can ever accomplish will top that distinction. Stand confident in your identity that begins and ends with Jesus so you can have clarity on what He has called you to do. You are precious in the sight of the Lord not because of your works but simply because you are His.

freedom + faith — our faith gives us freedom!

Peace.
Clarity.

> 66 ——
> *Titles fade, recognition is never constant, but who we are in Christ never waivers.*

TITUS
3:5

HE SAVED US, NOT BECAUSE
OF WORKS DONE BY US IN
RIGHTEOUSNESS BUT
ACCORDING TO
HIS OWN MERCY,
BY THE WASHING OF
REGENERATION AND
RENEWAL OF THE
HOLY SPIRIT.

3

FOR WHAT IT'S WORTH

"For you formed my inward parts; you knitted me together in my
mother's womb. I praise you, for I am fearfully and wonderfully made.
Wonderful are your works; my soul knows it very well."
Psalm 139:13-14 ESV

The phrase "you are worthy" is a powerful term that naturally evokes confidence within us. For a time, this phrase gained popularity among personal growth circles and was printed on mugs for some morning inspiration with your coffee. However, followers of Christ are left with some crucial questions regarding this statement. Where does our worthiness come from, and how do we measure it?

Our world measures our worth by the results we produce, the titles we hold, and the material possessions acquired. It can be tempting within the Social Selling industry to view someone's rank, the size of their team, or maybe their presence on a stage as an indicator of their worth or value. Thankfully, God does not measure us by the world's economy.

In 1 Timothy 1:15, Paul writes, "...that Christ Jesus came into the world to save sinners, of whom I am the foremost." Although our accomplishments, gifts, and talents can produce valuable outcomes, they can never fully capture our worth. Jesus made us invaluable when He rescued us from our sins. He alone is the only One worthy to bestow value upon us.

Take courage, friend, because our worthiness is first and foremost found in Christ, which should be a profound encouragement to all of us. That means we can give our best effort towards achieving our goals, but in the end, our worth to God does not change whether we succeed or fail.

We have had to cling to this truth through seasons of falling short in our business and countless failures. Human nature is to take on shame and believe we have nothing of worth to offer. But God, He is not the author of shame. The enemy prowls around like a roaring lion who would love to devalue your worth and render you useless for the Kingdom. If we attach our worth to the outcomes of our efforts, then we become prisoners to our circumstances.

Thankfully, when God looks down upon you, He is not evaluating your worthiness on how you perform. He does not hope you will get with the program, do better, or work harder. When God looks down upon you, He sees His perfect Son, Jesus Christ, within you and is well pleased.

There is so much freedom to be found, knowing our worth comes from Christ alone. Not just in our personal life but in business as well. Neither your back office, sales numbers, or the size of your team reflects your importance. The true reflection of your worth comes from Jesus; therefore, we can confidently pursue these other areas with complete freedom.

Canva graphic?

You are worthy.

You are worthy of love.

You are worthy of grace.

You are worthy of joy.

You are worthy to have purpose.

You are worthy to have dreams. What are Christ's dreams for us?

You are worthy of all these things because Christ within you is worthy. You are free to serve, love, and pursue your passions without the burden of trying to establish your worth through what you have achieved. Our accomplishments, though important, do not define us; our identity in Christ does.

So go live humbly as someone of great value and worth. ♥ Let your actions reflect the reality that though you were once unworthy due to sin, you deserve to be identified as full of worth because you have been forgiven. You are worthy because Christ within you is worthy. Now, go spread that worth to others.

Peace I give unto you... He gives us the gift of peace.

God created us w/ value. We are His creations. We are worthy bc He is worthy! Furthermore —

> " ——
> When God looks down upon you, He sees His perfect Son, Jesus Christ, within you and is well pleased.

Bc we chose Jesus.
↓
God is pleased w/ us!

now in Christ we are free from sin + worthy as He is worthy! He chose to redeem us bc He sees us valuable.

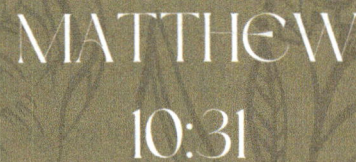

MATTHEW
10:31

FEAR NOT,
THEREFORE; YOU
ARE OF MORE
VALUE THAN MANY
SPARROWS.

4

THE ART OF REMEMBERING

*"I remember the days of old; I meditate on all that You have
done; I ponder the work of Your hands."*
Psalm 143:5 ESV

D o you remember where you were, or better yet, who you were when you first met Jesus? The longer we walk with Christ, the more we understand the vastness of the grace bestowed upon us. Jesus knew exactly who we are, with all of our transgressions past and future, yet He took our debt and made it His own. As we grow older, we realize that though trappings of sin may linger, the enormity of the cross is ever present to release the shackles.

As followers of Christ, it is healthy to take a moment to "look back" and remember all the things the Lord has done. Social Selling has been God's way of provision through the darkest financial season of our lives. Yet despite experiencing God's mighty hand time and again, we still wrestle with doubt and fear when walking through hard seasons.

It is almost like we have miracle memory loss. The devil likes to whisper in our ears, "God must not care about you because He is letting you suffer," or "You deserve this." Sometimes, we entertain those whispers until we believe them and forget the faithful goodness of our Heavenly Father.

The world is broken; we need not convince you of that reality. However, just because we live in a fallen world does not mean we cannot have confidence when facing trials along our path. Over the years, we have developed a practice called "the art of remembering," which is simply taking time to reflect on the faithfulness of God in our lives.

Psalm 143:5 states, "I remember the days of old; I meditate on all that you have done; I ponder the work of your hands." It is healthy for us to look back at what God has done so we can confidently face what lies ahead. As the psalmist observes, it is incredible to contemplate all that God has accomplished—whether it's sustaining us through the darkest moments, guiding us to mountaintop experiences, or instilling dreams and goals within our hearts.

Our identity in Jesus is not defined by our past but by His grace; along with that grace is the promise of a new beginning. We know that His grace finds us anew each day when we wake to breathe the free air the Gospel provides. That is a grace that is undeserved but is freely given by a good, good God.

With complete confidence and proof from our past, we can hold our heads up high to face whatever may come our way. The problem you may be facing today might seem insurmountable, but take heart that it did not take God by surprise, nor is this mountain too big for Him to move. With the constant pull on your soul to look forward, remember when.

Reflecting on God's provision in the past will ignite a deeper trust, knowing that He will continue to be faithful in the future because He is the same yesterday, today, and tomorrow. Israel would build monuments along their journey to commemorate what God did for them. We, too, have mental memorials that we can draw from that help us remember how God has shown up amid our trials time and time again.

If you are experiencing hardship in any aspect of life this season, take some time to practice the art of remembering. Pause and reflect on all that God has done, and have confidence that He did not forsake you back then, and He will not start now. As you ponder the works of God you have seen come to pass, be assured that He will continue to show up for you now and in the years to come.

> *What you are facing today seems insurmountable, but it did not take God by surprise nor is it too much for Him to handle.*

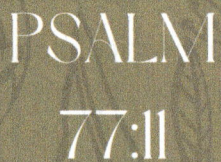

PSALM
77:11

I WILL REMEMBER THE
DEEDS OF THE LORD;
YES, I WILL
REMEMBER YOUR
WONDERS OF OLD.

5

COVENANT OVER CONTRACT

"But God shows his love for us in that while we were still sinners, Christ died for us."
Romans 5:8 ESV

We sold our house last year, and as many of you know, selling a home is not for the faint of heart. Moving with nine kids also presents unique challenges. However, keeping your house spotless as total strangers walk through it with white gloves is physically and mentally exhausting. Particularly when your realtor calls with a showing request, and the potential buyers want to be there in fifteen minutes!

After a few weeks on the market, a nice young family placed an offer on our house, and we began to sprint towards closing. Everything was going perfectly until the time of our inspection. Hearing the words from the inspector, "You have a lovely home… just needs a new roof," shocked us as we had not lived in the home long, and the roof seemed fine. So, we now found ourselves in a whirlwind of quotes, timelines, and even more prayer.

We had to have a new roof installed on the house for the buyers to continue with the purchase. One new roof later allowed both parties to fulfill the purchase contract, and we closed a beautiful chapter of our lives, moving on to a new calling and adventure.

Sometimes, we treat our relationship with God as if we are under a contract with Him. If we keep our lives clutter-free, presentable to the public and ensure the "roof" does not leak... then God will fulfill His side of the contract.

A contract relationship is the idea that if we perform in this life, God will surely love us. All we have to do is keep up our side of the bargain, and He will then keep up His.

The problem with approaching our relationship with God in a "contract" mentality is that contracts fall apart. If one side does not deliver what was promised, the other can walk away. If we had informed our buyers that we were unwilling to invest in a new roof, they would not have held up their side of the contract and would have walked away.

In a contract relationship, both parties bring something of value to the negotiating table so that both sides get what they want. Friends, it is different with God. We carry only our sins and brokenness to the table while God brings us His everything. He brings us His one and only Son.

Thankfully, we are not in a contract relationship with God but rather a covenant relationship. A covenant is a promise between ourselves and the Lord that is sealed by the life, death, and resurrection of Christ. We lay our sins out on the table, and God brings salvation. We bring nothing and yet leave with everything. We inherit a love with no strings attached, fostering a faith that the Covenant Maker will never walk away.

We will fail over and again, endlessly disappoint people, and never be able to live up to the standards the Lord has set for us. Nevertheless, our salvation with the Lord is not null and void. On our worst days, we can confidently stand because while we were yet sinners, Jesus died for us. We brought our brokenness to the table and exchanged it for wholeness that comes only from the work on the cross.

God's covenant with you remains steadfast, unaffected by what you bring to the table. Its unbreakable nature derives from who He is, not contingent on your offerings. The beautiful part of a covenant relationship versus a contract is that the Lord is the one who creates, validates, and sustains the agreement. Cling to that covenant, friend, for within this agreement is life everlasting.

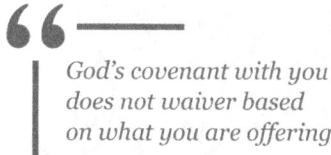

God's covenant with you does not waiver based on what you are offering.

HEBREWS
8:6

BUT AS IT IS, CHRIST HAS
OBTAINED A MINISTRY
THAT IS AS MUCH MORE
EXCELLENT THAN THE
OLD AS THE COVENANT
HE MEDIATES IS BETTER,
SINCE IT IS ENACTED ON
BETTER PROMISES.

6

FIND YOUR VOICE

"Then the Lord put out his hand and touched my mouth.
And the Lord said to me, "Behold, I have put my words in your mouth."
Jeremiah 1:9 ESV

As a young pastor, I listened to sermons from other preachers to be encouraged, inspired, and personally grow in my walk with the Lord. Following leaders in ministry that I admired taught me so much about preaching and leading from the pulpit. However, the most important lesson I learned from them came indirectly.

During the early era of my pastorate, a fellow pastor and good friend came to my church to hear me preach one Sunday morning. Afterward, we went out to lunch and discussed what was happening in each other's lives and ministries. I finally got enough courage to ask him about my sermon. I told him to give me all the constructive criticism he could muster.

With a sly smirk, my friend said, "You need to find your voice." I had no idea what he meant. Did I not speak loud enough? Was my voice too low? I was rerunning every word of my sermon through my head, wondering what possibly I could have said. He could see the confusion on my face. He laughed and said, "I can tell you listen to certain big-name pastors because you sound just like them. You need to find your voice. You don't need to sound like anyone else to be successful. God called you to speak to these people with your own voice. "

He was not accusing me of stealing sermons from other preachers. What he meant was that my cadence, my rhythms, and my language mimicked other famous pastors. He encouraged me to find my own voice because God had uniquely gifted me to reach my particular community.

My church did not need me to mirror someone else's voice meant for a different group. They needed me and my voice. They needed the words that God had bestowed upon me to proclaim.

To this day, that was some of the most remarkable advice I have ever received in ministry, and I have also applied it to Social Selling. You are who you are because that is how God created you. Your experiences, gifts, and personality are unique to you. He will use all that you are to impact people that He has already set aside for you to serve.

Your story, experiences, pain, failures, and growth are all purposed for such a time as this. Do not try to be something you are not. Show up as your most true, authentic self. Others can inspire you, but never lose the voice the Lord uniquely crafted for you.

You have something important to say, and your words matter to God and those He wants to hear them. You may not believe in your voice immediately, but with practice, you will find the words God wants you to proclaim. Finding your voice does not mean you say everything perfectly, but it does mean you can speak authentically from a heart that the Lord has molded.

Embrace your God-given personality. Whether you are a leader who loves to train from the stage or if you prefer to lead with quiet strength, be the person that God has uniquely created you to be. While we strive for growth, it's crucial not to lose who we are in the pursuit of progress. Your words matter, and your story is significant, even if it unfolds differently than you might have hoped.

As Jeremiah penned, you have words from the Lord to speak. So raise your voice. He has commissioned you for proclamation. You have a story to tell, Good News to proclaim, and a people to impact. Know your voice and use it because it is the one God has given you to make much of Him.

66 ——

Your gifts, your experiences, and your voice matter to God.

PSALM
19:14

LET THE WORDS OF MY
MOUTH AND THE
MEDITATION OF MY
HEART BE ACCEPTABLE
IN YOUR SIGHT,
O LORD, MY ROCK AND
MY REDEEMER.

7

NO COMPARISON

"For am I now seeking the approval of man, or of God? Or am I trying to please man? If I were still trying to please man, I would not be a servant of Christ."
Galatians 1:10 ESV

Comparison destroys all sense of contentment; it's the thief of joy along this beautiful journey. Yet, we frequently fall to this scheme of the enemy, leaving us feeling defeated and worthless. Comparison leads us to believe that we lack what others somehow possess.

The pitfalls of comparison breed envy, jealousy, and strife, yet beneath these emotions lies a more profound concern—our dissatisfaction. We engage in comparison because we are discontent with the path God has set for us and lack trust in His intended journey for our lives.

The tendency to compare often fuels an unhealthy desire to deviate from our God-ordained story and adopt a narrative that is not our own. It is heightened within entrepreneurship as we are surrounded by others who are also running towards similar business goals.

We compare the speed of our journey, the skills or giftings we seem to be missing, our struggle to cast vision, etc.... the comparison game goes on and on. Rather than seeing progress as a victory, our perception of what we lack distorts all the beauty of what we already possess.

The prevalence of social media has heightened the temptation to compare all the more. A mere few minutes of scrolling can lead us into a spiral of defeat, leaving us paralyzed to show up authentically. We find ourselves contrasting the highlight moments of others with the ordinary aspects of our daily lives.

Paul proposes a vital question in the first chapter of Galatians for entrepreneurs and followers of Christ. Who are we serving? Whom are we trying to impress? What is the end goal of our efforts? If we are seeking the approval of others, then we will be caught in a vicious cycle of comparison. The Lord sees that you are working hard and your activity is not in vain, but all too often, we lose sight of our own journey when we begin to compare our journey to someone else's.

Comparison takes us away from walking our path to sitting on the sidelines, spectating someone else's expedition. Comparison reveals that we are not satisfied with the road God has for us but that we desire a different route, for it seems shorter, more accessible, or more scenic than ours.

God has set you on a unique journey, unlike anyone else's. He is aware of the steps you will take, the experiences you will encounter, the obstacles you will overcome, and the victories you will achieve. There is no need to compare yourself to others when you trust in the Lord, who is beyond comparison.

The Lord has equipped you for the adventure ahead, with all its highs and lows. We serve Him, no matter what may come, because we know this place is not our home. Heaven is coming.

When we witness the success of others, we can genuinely celebrate their achievements when we recognize that they are navigating the path the Lord has designed for them, just as we are on our unique journey. While we are all on different routes and timelines, the ultimate purpose is the same. The glory of God. Show up and run your race. Stay the course. Your faithfulness will impact the lives of others for a Kingdom purpose.

66 ——

God has equipped you for the adventure ahead, with all it's highs and lows, so we must keep looking forward.

GALATIANS
6:4

BUT LET EACH ONE TEST
HIS OWN WORK, AND
THEN HIS REASON TO
BOAST WILL BE IN
HIMSELF ALONE AND
NOT IN HIS NEIGHBOR.

HOLY CALLING

8

THE INVITATION

"And Jesus came and said to them, "All authority in heaven and on earth has been given to me. Go therefore and make disciples of all nations, baptizing them in the name of the Father and of the Son and of the Holy Spirit, teaching them to observe all that I have commanded you. And behold, I am with you always, to the end of the age."
Matthew 28: 18-20 ESV

When your soul was relieved from sin through faith in Jesus, you were not just set free from transgressions, but you were invited into the very presence of God. There is power in that invitation. Our life laid bare in front of the Creator of everything, with our shortcomings on full display, and yet He invites us to be His beloved child. The invitation is not earned based on our own merit but rather a gift of God's grace alone.

Jesus, in Matthew 28:11, invites any who are weary and carrying heavy burdens to come near. He calls us to draw near. He offers us rest. Our faith is a result of the greatest invitation, the Gospel. Now we can tell others they are welcomed too, finding rest from sin that weighs them down.

Jesus tells the disciples in Matthew 28:18-20 that, first and foremost, "all authority" has been given to Him. This includes the calling of our life. The impact we will make. The mission we are to pursue. The way we will live our lives. The authority over all these things has been granted to Him. God dictates our call to "go and make disciples" and what that call will look like.

Jesus continues in Matthew that we are to "go" and make disciples. We are to actively invite people into a relationship with Jesus. Even though we do none of the work that leads to transformation, we are vessels in sharing the transforming message. Christ invites us to the work of discipling, and there is power in that invitation.

Notice how Jesus does not designate how we are to go. All we know is that we are supposed to reach all the nations with the message of Christ, but He does not specify how we are to proclaim this message. Many of us have used our vocation, interests, and relationships to broadcast the message of Jesus to others. With endless avenues for the Gospel to go forth, we believe that your Social Selling business is an incredible platform for the Kingdom.

You are not just a representative or partner with your company. You are an ambassador for Christ, and you are using your vocation to "go and make disciples."

We know that to be successful in this industry, you must share what your company offers. Sharing more can lead to business success, but when Kingdom minded you can build your business towards a deeper significance.

Your business can be a means to fulfill Jesus' command to GO and make disciples. If we are a "go and tell" faith, take assurance that you can do just that through this platform.

In Matthew 28 Jesus invites us to participate in the making of disciples, which is transformational for the hearer of the gospel and for us who are on mission. Jesus frees us from sin but also invites us to a mission.

Your calling is so much bigger than achieving a rank, earning incentives or increasing your paycheck. Not that God cannot be honored in those things, but the impact we make in the lives of others on this side of heaven far outweighs any earthly reward we can achieve.

We have the privilege to transform people's lives for eternity with the Gospel. To go and invite others to personally know their Savior. It just so happens that God, for this season, has provided you a platform with your business as the "how" to further His mission and live out our calling.

When we are invited to encounter Jesus, like John and Peter in Acts 4:20, we cannot help but go and tell what we have seen and heard from our experience with Christ. So friends, today, go. Invite. Not just an invitation into your company but into a relationship that can lead to transformation through Christ.

> 66 ——
> *Your calling is so much bigger than ranking up, making money, and earning incentives.*

ACTS
1:8

BUT YOU WILL RECEIVE
POWER WHEN THE HOLY
SPIRIT HAS COME UPON
YOU, AND YOU WILL BE MY
WITNESS IN JERUSALEM
AND IN ALL JUDEA AND
SAMARIA, AND TO THE END
OF THE EARTH.

9

WHO YOU ARE BECOMING

"Therefore, my beloved, as you have always obeyed, so now, not only as in my presence but much more in my absence, work out your own salvation with fear and trembling, for it is God who works in you, both to will and to work for his good pleasure."
Philippians 2:12-13 ESV

Courage is not always the will to take a leap of faith or to muster the bravery to face daunting challenges. Sometimes courage is just listening to that small voice deep inside that says, "Tomorrow is a new day." That will to keep going and assurance in God's calling over our lives creates confidence to embrace obstacles.

Within this industry, we are often faced with the need to learn new skills, develop as leaders, and grow in our mindset. Many come up against these obstacles and walk away because their growth is uncomfortable. Thankfully, we serve a God who gives us growth opportunities because He cares about who we are and is deeply concerned about who we will become.

As believers, our calling has no real ending but is a lifetime of working out our purpose daily. It is answering a call to grow into a disciple of Jesus that reflects His character and nature. Our calling from God is not just about what we do but about who we become in the process.

Pursuing your calling can be challenging, but it is always worth answering. We can remember when we felt God moving us out of pastoral ministry and into a new season of entrepreneurship. That stirring was filled with many emotions, specifically fear and doubt that we could not do what God called us to. However, the Lord made it evident that He does not call the qualified but rather qualifies the called. He wasn't calling us to this because of who we were but rather because He has so much more growth for us to experience.

The obedience to the call would bring refinement to our lives and a new way to "work out our salvation," as Paul states in Philippians. Social Selling would be our new pulpit/platform, our customers/team would be the people we would shepherd, and the gospel we had preached for years would now find a new way to be proclaimed.

We knew this shift from pastoring to full-time entrepreneurs in Social Selling would require us to grow in areas we were not fully confident in. That is what God's calling does. Removing you from comfort into a space where you can rely on God in deeper ways.

It will challenge you to reach new heights in your activity and faith to make a more resounding impact on the world around you. God's ways are not our ways, and so He knows the very thing needed that will refine us in our faith and character.

God has not set you aside in this industry just to be successful. He has set you aside to grow and shape you. Though it will take courage, if we genuinely pursue God's calling, it is impossible for us not to grow in faith and character.

God never calls those who are fully equipped to fulfill His will. He is looking for something other than the perfect business mind, the flawless leader, or the savvy marketer. God is looking for a willing vessel to spread the good news of Christ.

Lean into your calling today and trust that voice in your heart that is beckoning you to do great things, even when those things are hard, scary, uncomfortable, and require us to grow. Trust that God is working within you and cares deeply about who you are becoming. God's call on your life sometimes feels like we are lost, but that's simply because it's uncomfortable. He is doing a great work within you, and who you will become will look more like Jesus than who you once were.

66 ——

Pursuing your calling can be challenging, but it is always worth answering.

2 TIMOTHY
1:9

WHO SAVED US AND
CALLED US TO A HOLY
CALLING, NOT BECAUSE OF
OUR WORKS BUT BECAUSE
OF HIS OWN
PURPOSE AND GRACE,
WHICH HE GAVE US IN
CHRIST JESUS BEFORE
THE AGES BEGAN.

10

WORKMANSHIP

For we are his workmanship, created in Christ Jesus for good works,
which God prepared beforehand, that we should walk in them.
Ephesians 2:10 ESV

You are not God's project. You are not some fading interest that He pays attention to from time to time. You are not something He pulls from the shelf, dusts off, and decides to work on when He can get around to it. You are God's "workmanship," and the Lord will never tire in crafting who we are to be in Christ.

Like a sculptor who can see the masterpiece that lies within the stone. Like a painter who sees more than just a blank canvas. Our God, the ultimate Creator, can behold the masterpiece of His Son within us that He wants to call forth and display for His glory.

When Christ redeems us, we are proclaimed as God's 'workmanship,' as Ephesians 2:10 declares. In this ongoing process, God actively shapes, molds, and refines us into His masterpiece. We are His unfinished creation, a work of art that He continues to craft, and this transformative journey extends until we meet Him face-to-face in heaven. Through His unwavering presence, abundant provision, and divine providence, we are intricately fashioned as His ongoing masterpiece.

Liberated to engage in righteous deeds in the name of Jesus, as you actively participate in these works, you are at the same time being crafted by God into someone who reflects the characteristics of Christ. Those we impact with these predetermined good works look not to praise the created but the Creator, the Master Craftsman whose glory can be seen through His handiwork.

Reading Ephesians 2:10, we can picture our lives laid out on a divine woodshop table. We can observe all the places where the Lord has smoothed out our rough surfaces, cleaned up our edges, and sanded down our shortcomings. He has set aside good works for His workmanship to participate in but is still constantly molding us more into the likeness of Christ.

Social Selling is simply another refining experience where God will continue to work out your purpose in making disciples. Though it may not meet your own plans that you once had, rest assured that the good works you are doing are not just for the benefit of others but to grow you closer to the Lord.

In an industry that promotes servanthood and customer care, we are positioned perfectly as Social Sellers to engage in these good works that God has set for us.

You can walk confidently in activity, knowing that God has set aside people for you to impact. It is comforting to know that there is someone even now waiting to encounter your story. Someone needing to hear about the hope that you possess.

We have witnessed so many opportunities to do good works within Social Selling that, on reflection, it is evident they were prepared beforehand by the Lord. We can hardly fathom the countless times we have been placed in a position to do good for others solely because God called us into this industry.

Friends, you are God's workmanship that was created in Christ. Be confident that He that began a great work in you will continue until it is finished.

So move forward in your calling with an unshakable faith, knowing that you were meant to walk in these good works that the Lord has gone forth and set aside just for you.

His masterpiece. His work of art. His workmanship.

We can walk confidently in our activity knowing that God has set aside people for us to impact.

2 CORINTHIANS 9:8

AND GOD IS ABLE TO
MAKE ALL GRACE
ABOUND TO YOU, SO
THAT HAVING ALL
SUFFICIENCY IN ALL
THINGS AT ALL TIMES,
YOU MAY ABOUND IN
EVERY GOOD WORK.

11

MOTIVES & MISSION

"Do not be conformed to this world, but be transformed by the renewal of your mind, that by testing you may discern what is the will of God, what is good and acceptable and perfect."
Romans 2:10 ESV

Maybe it was that passive comment from a friend, questioning how you could join a Direct Sales company. Or maybe it's the small voice in the back of your head that tells you to shamefully give up. Where you once were confident, you now question if you can indeed be on a mission to make disciples through the platform of your business.

What you are asking, what most Christian Social Sellers are truly longing for, is to be confident that your business motives also align with God's mission. Our love for Christ compels us to desire alignment between this passion for pursuing goals in this industry while also bearing fruit for the Kingdom.

Romans 12:2 says our minds are transformed by the renewal that Jesus brings. If God has transformed our minds, we can conclude that our pursuits, goals, and motivations can also be reset to reflect the glory of God. We can trust that God is also the author of the dreams and visions placed within our hearts. With a renewed mind in Christ, we inherit a transformative perspective on what really matters.

Romans 8:6 states, "The mind governed by the Spirit is life and peace." When God's Word reinforces our motives, vision, and heart, we gain confidence in our calling and motivations. Our motives are no longer controlled by worldly ambition but by Christ-centered regeneration.

As we stated on day one of this devotional, many who read these pages want to find peace in their Social Selling business. There is a desire for assurance that you are in God's will concerning your business. Friends, if the Spirit governs your mind and Christ rules your heart, you can have peace as you run with wild abandonment towards your dreams.

You are not in this industry by accident, chance, or serendipity. In our opinion, those things do not even exist due to God's sovereignty. God is using the people in this industry to further His Kingdom and provide for His people.

The boundless love of Christ should be the driving force behind all our endeavors. As we step into the realm of Social Selling, love must stand as our paramount motivator and chief source of joy. While expanding your team may boost your financial gains, it becomes even more significant as it amplifies your opportunity to share the profound love of Christ with others. Remember, your efforts extend beyond worldly comforts; you are laboring on behalf of Jesus, driven by a purpose that transcends mere material success.

What is motivating you? Are you in this industry for fame, comfort, and to experience an abundance of wealth? Or are you in this industry because you are called to provide for your family, serve others, and help people experience the abundant life we share in Christ?

My friends, your mind and heart are where your motives live. With a renewed mind and heart comes new motivations that look nothing like the world but instead look like a holy ambition pleasing to God.

Aligning our hearts with God's mission means we have filtered our motivations through Christ. Through this renewing process of our minds, we can discern which of our activities align with God's mission and which fall outside of His will.

Your motivations as a Social Seller can complement God's mission to redeem all of Creation. That motivating desire for you to succeed is not just for the benefit of your financial situation but can also be for the betterment of those the Lord wants to transform.

> **"**
> *Our motives are no longer controlled by worldly ambition but by Christ-centered regeneration.*

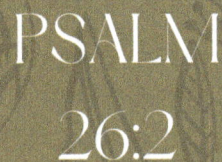

PSALM
26:2

PROVE ME,
O LORD
AND TRY ME;
TEST MY HEART
AND MY MIND.

12

DIVINE PARTNERSHIP

"Our God is in the heavens; He does all that He pleases."
Psalm 115:3 ESV

uffering is an all too familiar companion in this life. Sometimes the cry for help is muffled from the weight of the world. Friend, know that even in your silence, the Lord hears your cries and will answer.

We all wish we knew the why behind the trials we face and when they will end. The simple truth is that while we may not comprehend the entirety of our suffering, our Heavenly Father does. Despite our earnest desire to make sense of certain situations, we can trust that the Lord knows every detail that is unfolding in our lives.

There are times we can trace back through the circumstances that led us to these challenging times and come to some conclusions about how we arrived at this difficult season. However, often we do not know. Even when we do not gain insight into our situations, the Lord has relentlessly assured us that He is still working on our behalf despite our understanding. We are in a divine partnership with Him, and our trust is well-founded.

In the past, we have lamented to each other that we have been "doing all the things" in our business but still did not achieve the results we were hoping for. Why did we not hit our goal? Why has God not seen fit for us to cross this certain threshold in our business? We don't know, but we believe it will make sense one day.

Understanding why we sometimes fall short of our goals may not always be evident. Yet, as we embrace our calling and recall the initial purpose that propelled us on this journey, we forge a divine partnership with God. In this connection, we trust that our current position is precisely where we are meant to be. Admittedly, leaning into this partnership is not always a straightforward path, but when we muster the courage to do so, the outcome never fails to be rewarding.

Our partnership with God is not based on Him delivering success to us in everything we attempt. It is trusting that God is in the heavens, as Psalm 115:3 states, and does all that pleases Him. Since we trust that what pleases God is always good for us, we can gladly partner with Him as He orchestrates every situation.

Whether you are in a stagnant season in your business or in a time of personal trials, though you may not understand why things are unfolding the way we are, we can trust that the Lord has not left us to our own devices. Our partnership with God is sealed by the Holy Spirit and guaranteed by our faith in Christ.

You are not alone if you feel like you have been doing everything you should be doing in your business, but your efforts are not producing the results you desire. We promise you are not the only person facing certain hardships. It can be frustrating and cause us to doubt our calling. However, God is still in the heavens, my friend. He has not left or forsaken you even when what we desire does not come to fruition.

He is still doing all that He pleases, and what He pleases is always good for us, even when we don't understand it. What we can know is that nothing happens without God's knowledge or permission.

Find comfort in, "I don't know, but one day it will make sense." That mentality is not putting your head in the sand. It's not willingly denying reality. It is simply trusting that you have partnered with the God of the heavens, who has presided over all that we have known or ever will know.

> **"**
> *We don't have to know everything because we partner with a God that does.*

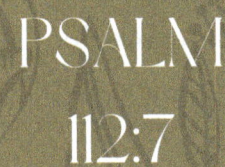

PSALM
112:7

HE IS NOT AFRAID
OF BAD NEWS;
HIS HEART IS FIRM,
TRUSTING IN THE
LORD.

13

THE WAY OF LOVE

"If I speak in the tongues of men and of angels, but have not love, I am a noisy
gong or a clanging cymbal. And if I have prophetic powers, and understand all
mysteries and all knowledge, and if I have all faith, so as to remove mountains,
but have not love, I am nothing. If I give away all I have, and if I deliver up my
body to be burned, but have not love, I gain nothing."
1st Corinthians 13:1-3 ESV

They love well.

Regardless of the many stages you may walk on or the accolades next to your name you during your Social Selling career, the ultimate measure of effectiveness lies in whether or not we love others well. The opportunity to love others brings an infinite reward that cannot be matched by any finite honor.

The highest commendation one can receive is to be recognized as someone who excels in serving others with no strings attached. Beyond any external recognition, the truest validation rests in being acknowledged for your capacity to extend genuine and meaningful love.

Regardless of business achievements, it's the leaders who love well that make the most lasting impression. Maya Angelou said, "I've learned that people will forget what you said, people will forget what you did, but people will never forget how you made them feel." As followers of Christ, we have such an incredible opportunity in this industry to help others feel the love Christ has for them.

1 Corinthians 13 has a powerful message, though it is often only ever recited at weddings. We all know verse 13, "...faith, hope, and love abide, these three; but the greatest of these is love." However, spend some time reading this chapter's first few verses, for they set up our heart position, which is critical in our lives and work.

A heart position of leading with love is a way to do business in a manner worthy of your calling. Our approach to Social Selling, as followers of Christ, should have distinct characteristics that set us apart. We ought to navigate this industry guided by love so that all we can point back to the love of Christ as the source.

Paul states at the beginning of 1 Corinthians 13 that even if you have the gift of speaking or vision casting but do not have love... you are a clanging gong that makes plenty of noise but contains little substance.

If you have faith, belief, and gifts but do not follow the way of love, then your efforts are meaningless. In other words, if you are generous with your time, resources, and sacrifice for others but do so without love, you will have gained nothing.

Do not miss this. Love is the overarching force that drives your business. It is the essential leadership skill to express when serving your team. 1 Corinthians 16:14 says, "Let all that you do be done with love."All that you do. Every post. Reach out. Conversation. Training. Lead with love.

One of the greatest misses would be to do all of this void of love. Does it even matter what we accomplish or how often we are recognized for our efforts if we are not leading with love? Not at all. For with love, our efforts will go out with a lasting impact far beyond anything temporal.

To work in the way of love, you must first experience that love from Jesus. His love for you is unwavering, not based on your daily performance but on His unfailing grace. When we experience and implement that love in our business, our return is much greater than our investment.

You are called to do great things, but those things will only truly matter if the love of Christ is at the center of your efforts. So, use your gifts and your talents to move towards your goals. Embrace your calling in this industry, but do so with Christ's love imprinted on every aspect of the business. For people will come and go. Our achievements will be celebrated and will fade away. However, to be remembered as someone who loved well will echo through generations.

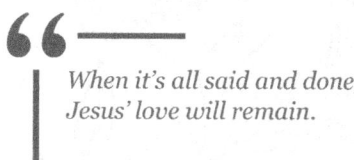

When it's all said and done, Jesus' love will remain.

1 CORINTHIANS
13:7

LOVE BEARS ALL THINGS,
BELIEVES ALL THINGS,
HOPES ALL THINGS,
ENDURES ALL THINGS.

14

MIRACLES IN THE MARGINS

"Do not withhold good from those to whom it is due,
when it is in your power to do it."
Proverbs 3:27 ESV

*E*very day holds the potential for miraculous moments. We serve a God whose works are so extraordinary that they defy earthly reasoning to those who have not yet encountered Him.

The profound reality that we are forgiven and embraced by God through Christ represents the most remarkable miracle any of us will ever experience. The miraculous should be common for followers of Jesus if we look for them not just in the grand moments of life but in our everyday interactions with others.

Turning our hearts away from earthly treasures that our business can store up and instead towards making eternal impacts upon the people we are able to serve. Showing up daily in your business as a vessel to be used by God is where the miracles unfold. The seemingly mundane activities that build our business is where God often shows up with transformation.

These miracles in the margins keep us in a constant state of wonder and awe of the redemptive power of the Lord. As Social Sellers dedicated to Jesus, our orientation toward miracles is heightened because our primary call is to be the hands and feet of Jesus to others.

The works of God can show up in the big moments, like walking out onto a stage in front of thousands, but the everyday miracles in the margins are those that are etched in our hearts forever.

It may be in a conversation with a friend who needs encouragement so that she may be able to get through their day. It may be the mom who needs so desperately to make a little more income to take the financial pressure off her family. It could simply be a message of care to someone who, unbeknownst to anyone, is having a hard day. Miracles can happen in the most common of interactions. What may seem like our "job" is actually our mission to bring genuine transformation.

Proverbs 3:27 urges us to do good for others when it is in our power to do so and not withhold blessings if possible. In small actions of care or grand gestures of servanthood, we should pour ourselves out like a drink offering.

It may seem like you are only making a marginal difference in someone's life, but for them, it could be the very miracle they have been praying for. Every small act, no matter how simple, plays a part in a grand design orchestrated by the Lord. So, as we build our businesses, let's remember that our actions can have a more significant impact than we realize and that God's plan unfolds in the everyday moments.

Your calling in Social Selling cannot begin and end with your happiness. To be truly fulfilled in this calling, it has to include impacting others both in small and extraordinary ways.

The everyday acts of service to others are the building blocks of the incredible calling the Lord has entrusted to you, allowing you to make a lasting impact on people. While the grand moments of rank-ups will be awe-inspiring, and the moments of recognition will bring satisfaction. It's the miracles woven into the intricate details of our business that are the ones that will be indelibly etched in our memories for a lifetime.

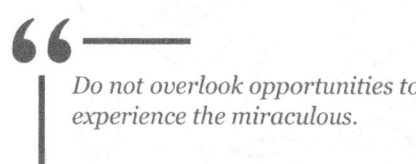

Do not overlook opportunities to experience the miraculous.

JOHN 14:12

TRULY, TRULY I SAY TO YOU, WHOEVER BELIEVES IN ME WILL ALSO DO THE WORKS THAT I DO; AND GREATER WORKS THAN THESE WILL HE DO, BECAUSE I AM GOING TO THE FATHER.

HOLY ACTION

15

SHOW UP

*"Therefore, my beloved brothers, be steadfast,
immovable, always abounding in the work of the Lord,
knowing that in the Lord your labor is not in vain"*
1st Corinthians 15:8 ESV

Our oldest biological son, Noah, is an incredible gift to our family and one of our greatest heroes. At 18 months, Noah was diagnosed with Autism, and we were told he may never speak or live independently. However, Noah has defied the odds and overcome every statistic he was labeled with. He is one of the kindest young men you will ever meet and will graduate high school next year and head off to college.

One day, driving home from errands, Noah shared that a few guys at school were "joking around" with him about his Autism. We could tell right away that Noah was experiencing bullying, but he was not willing to label it so harshly. I wish I could say that this was the first time, but unfortunately, this has been a regular occurrence for him over the years.

I was about to go into one of my dad speeches where I remind him that God gave him unique gifts and encourage him to speak up. All the while, I was trying to hide the fact that I was furious that he was experiencing this kind of treatment once again.

Noah stated before I could say a word, "But you know, I still show up for myself no matter what they say because I like who I am." It is incredible how, out of nowhere, kids courageously speak with such wisdom. Noah smiled out the window, signaling that the problem was resolved and that he did not need me to remind him how special he was.

Like Noah, I think God wants us to show up in our daily lives, not just for ourselves but for others. Even when it is hard, showing up is an admittance that even when we may struggle to carry on, by God's strength, we will.

1 Corinthians 5:18 has always been a guiding verse for me, especially when the impulse to retreat arises. Paul's charge to be "steadfast" and "immovable" paints a beautiful picture, instilling the confidence to stand tall in the face of opposition.

There will inevitably be moments when the inclination is to do anything else but show up. Doubts about the significance of our efforts may arise, and the opinions of others might tempt us to withdraw. In those challenging moments or seasons, we must heed Paul's counsel by remaining steadfast and immovable, our focus fixed on Jesus.

In times of struggle, it's crucial to reflect on the divine calling in our lives, recognizing that our actions hold significance. The only actual defeat comes when we choose not to show up. When we refuse to show up, we are denying others of our efforts and what God wants to do for them through us.

Today, my friend, stand resolute in your purpose, unwavering in your convictions, as your labor is not solely for personal gain but for the Lord. Regardless of whether the results align with your expectations, your toil is not in vain.

Even in moments when comprehending this truth proves challenging, whether through sight, feeling, or understanding, rest assured that your work is never futile. The work you abound in, within your business or personal life, is making a difference to someone.

Noah shows up for himself every day because he understands that his purpose is more significant than his comfort. It is greater than the opinions of others who cannot recognize his gifts. Noah is steadfast and immovable in his purpose even though he has valid excuses to hide away from the world. Nonetheless, he shows up because his presence abounds in the work that the Lord wants to do.

Show up today, friends, even when you would rather hide, for your labor has meaning. Your efforts for the Lord will not be wasted.

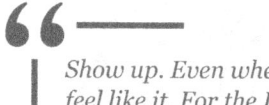

Show up. Even when you don't feel like it. For the Lord will not let you labor in vain.

HEBREWS
6:10

FOR GOD IS NOT
UNJUST SO AS TO
OVERLOOK YOUR
WORK AND THE
LOVE THAT YOU HAVE
SHOWN FOR HIS NAME
IN SERVING THE SAINTS,
AS YOU STILL DO.

16

PRESENCE NOT PERFECTION

"Brothers, I do not consider that I have made it my own.
But one thing I do: forgetting what lies behind and straining
forward to what lies ahead, I press on toward the goal for the
prize of the upward call of God in Christ Jesus."
Philippians 3:13-14 ESV

The relentless pursuit of perfection often ends in defeat and disappointment. It is an ideal that is elusive and unattainable, leaving a wake of destruction in its path.

Chasing after perfectionism has the potential to alienate others, as they may struggle to keep pace, or it can compel you to withdraw, unable to present an authentic picture of real life. If we can embrace that progress is the goal, then we can be present for ourselves and others, finding beauty in our shared inadequacies.

A few years ago, we were on a call with our business coach, sharing how we weren't showing up for our team because we did not feel we were "good enough" leaders. For that matter, we did not always feel enough for our family, each other, and our relationships. After our lament, she said, "You do not need to be perfect in all these areas; you just need to be present." Our coach spent the rest of the session reminding us that the people we care about in our lives love us for who we are, not that we show up perfectly.

Our perfection, or lack thereof, does not influence them to keep moving forward in their efforts. They are not hoping for perfection; they want us to be present in their lives because it brings value to them.

Philippians 3:13-14 talks about striving towards the calling God has granted us through Christ. That call should be so powerful in our lives that we leave behind past failures. We move forward knowing that the grace of God has paved the way for us to continue.

Ecclesiastes 9:10 notes that whatever we put our hands to work on, we should do so with our most significant effort. Being released from the constant striving frees us to give our full effort with great compassion. Psalm 90:17 states that the Lord will establish our work.

God established your work here in this space. Don't hide your humanity by wrapping it up with a perfect bow. The best leaders are those that are present, not perfect. Showing that fear and failure are a part of the journey and that there is no shame in the struggle. Create a culture that celebrates showing up just as you are yet working towards growth at the same time.

There will never be a time when we "arrive" as a leader, a spouse, a parent, a friend, or any other area of our lives because we are broken humans. Thankfully, we are covered by grace, and there is always room for growth.

As Paul states in Philippians 3, we strive forward, not slowed down by past failures. We press towards the goal, the upward call of God, knowing that is the true prize of our faithfulness.

Our pursuit should not be to reach perfection but to be present in the work, relationships, and goals the Lord has beckoned us to chase after. There was one perfect person who walked the earth. You and I are not Him. Praise the Lord. So may we not let past failures where we have fallen short of perfection stop us from being present today.

Do not let past failures or the need for perfection stop you from being present today.

PROVERBS
16:3

COMMIT YOUR
WORK TO THE LORD,
AND YOUR WILL
PLANS BE
ESTABLISHED.

17

CREATED TO WORK

*"The Lord God took the man and put him in the
garden of Eden to work it and keep it."*
Genesis 2:15 ESV

God created you for work. The stirring inside of you to create, build, and work is not selfish or sinful but was placed there by the Lord. As Genesis 2:15 notes, we are mandated to cultivate the earth and labor where God has placed whe

The word "cultivate" in this passage comes from the Hebrew word to serve or work. God's intentions for humanity were to engage in this cultural mandate of work to maintain or "keep" the things around him while also helping them flourish.

God gives the command to cultivate before sin entered into the world, meaning work is not a punishment for our sin; it's part of God's design.

You may grapple with the notion of work, fearing it may take you away from the roles God has bestowed upon you. Friends, whether you dedicate twenty minutes or hours each day to work, you can honor God through your efforts and still be present as a parent and spouse.

The notion of work does not have to conform to the world's conventional definition. As believers, our work encompasses serving, keeping, and cultivating what God has placed in your hands so that you can glorify God.

We see the woman of God described in Proverbs 31 by Solomon as one who works yet and at the same time praised by her family. Proverbs 31:24 states, "She makes linen garments and sells them; she delivers sashes to the merchant," and continues in verse 31, "Give her the fruit of her hands, and let her works praise her in the gates."

When God created us to work, we were designed to use our gifts and provide for our family's needs. The very design of work is God given and designed to cultivate impact for the Kingdom.

When we listen to the enemy's lies of the design of work instead of God's voice, we will grow stagnant in our activity and lose focus of the vision the Lord has given us. We do not work to gain recognition or rewards. Rather, we work to provide for our families, create opportunities, serve others, and exercise our gifts because whatever we do is to bring glory to God.

Work was never meant to become our identity, idol, or escape. It is a tool for impact and ministry in the marketplace.

Talk with your loved ones about your rhythms of work. Set boundaries that feel right for everyone in this specific season. Make a promise to be open to communication and feedback.

Friends, as with all good things created by God, the enemy likes to take it and deceptively twist it. Stand firm that your work is a tool of holy activity to bring glory to God. Take on the mandate given to us in the beginning. Work to serve, to create, and bring glory to the Lord.

Let's remove the lies the enemy whispers in our ears and replace those thoughts with a Christ-centered mindset:

Lie: You are all about prizes and money.
Truth: *I am motivated to serve people.*

Lie: You are all about self-promotion.
Truth: *I am all about promoting Christ.*

Lie: You want to live a life of abundance.
Truth: *I want to live an abundant life in Jesus.*

Lie: You will neglect your family if you work.
Truth: *I will support my family and be more present even in my call to work.*

Work should not be used as a means of escape but as a tool for marketplace ministry.

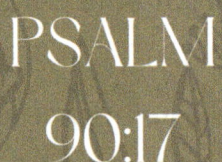

PSALM
90:17

LET THE FAVOR OF THE
LORD OUR GOD BE
UPON US, AND
ESTABLISH THE WORK
OF OUR HANDS UPON
US; YES, ESTABLISH THE
WORK OF OUR HANDS!

18

LIVING WITNESS

"Only let your manner of life be worthy of the gospel of Christ, so that whether I come and see you or am absent, I may hear of you that you are standing firm in one spirit, with one mind striving side by side for the faith of the gospel..."
Philippians 1:27 ESV

As much as our actions hold significance, so does the impact of our testimony. Christian Social Sellers often grapple with the fear of what others might think about them. Unlike professions such as teaching or nursing, the direct sales industry often triggers concerns about the image we project, as our names become linked directly to the products or services we represent.

It's crucial to understand that the industry itself doesn't dictate others' opinions of our character; rather, it's the manner in which we conduct our business that shapes perceptions. Our daily choices carry significant weight, reflecting our Christian witness.

A few years ago, we were having dinner with a new friend who had just been hired on the corporate side of the company we partner with. He had previously worked in a different industry for a larger company, and we could not help but ask him why he made the transition. Unapologetically, he said, "My previous company just wanted to win, no matter the costs, and my values simply could not align with a company like that."

What he had to say about his past experiences took us by surprise. His conviction over being able to work in a manner that aligned with his morals was so firm that he was willing to walk away from an auspicious career and start anew.

In Philippians 1:27, we are asked to have our lives portrayed in a manner that is "worthy of the gospel." We learn from this passage that a way of life worthy of the Gospel brings steadfastness, unity, and partnership. The activity of "living" that Paul calls us to is not the work that brings salvation. It's the work that follows it.

Having been redeemed and now resting in the love of the Savior, your actions should mirror the transformation that comes with encountering Christ's grace. In our daily business endeavors, living a life that authentically reflects our redemption with Jesus and the gospel's transformative power will alleviate concerns about perception. We are not entrepreneurs driven solely by a "win at all costs" mentality; we are servants committed to embodying a love-at-all-cost outlook.

In the passage mentioned, Paul emphasizes that whether he is physically present or absent from the Philippians, he desires to hear of their unity and witness a manner of life that clearly reflects the imprint of the transformative power of the good news of Christ. The conduct of our lives, including our business actions, should primarily convey to others that we have encountered the Living God.

You may fear that others are questioning why you went into Social Selling. You may worry that your character has taken a hit due 'to other people's preconceived notions or judgment. However, the confidence in our calling to pursue a business in this industry comes from the Lord and not the opinion of others. We live for an audience of One, knowing He will work in and through our obedience to Him.

Your worthiness in this industry is not derived from your expertise, success, or natural ability; it springs from the transformative power of Jesus.

May your activity in your business be holy so that you may be a witness to people who desperately need what you have discovered. The Gospel has completely transformed you; now it's time to live a life reflecting that truth in our daily life and business.

We are not "win at all costs" entrepreneurs, rather we are "love at all costs servants."

1 THESSALONIANS 4:1

FINALLY, THEN, BROTHERS, WE ASK AND URGE YOU IN THE LORD JESUS, THAT AS YOU RECEIVED FROM US HOW YOU OUGHT TO WORK AND TO PLEASE GOD, JUST AS YOU ARE DOING, THAT YOU DO SO MORE AND MORE.

19

SIGNIFICANCE OVER SUCCESS

"Do nothing from selfish ambition or conceit, but in humility count others more significant than yourselves. Let each of you look not only to his own interests, but also to the interests of others."
Philippians 2:3-4 ESV

The world is obsessed with success. The rise of social media has made this reality even more apparent as we weigh our "likes" and "shares" and the ever-elusive hope to go "viral." We are conditioned to believe that the more success achieved, the more significant that person becomes.

In Social Selling, that belief can shape how we show up in our business. May we be vigilant to protect our minds from the world's version of success. Sadly, we've watched the torment that comes from clawing toward success and recognition as people trample upon one another in order to get ahead.

No matter how much is achieved, success will always be fleeting if it is not tied to making a significant impact in the lives of others. The cheers begin to vanish, the congratulatory comments fade, and unfulfillment settles deep when success is the measuring stick.

Chasing success can be one of the most destructive races you'll ever run. It ends with broken dreams and a lifetime of regret. Success without significance is meaningless.

Without significance, we ask questions like, "Why do I feel numb at this moment?" or "I feel exhausted and burnt out," and we begin to wonder why we are even showing up anymore. To fight this empty feeling, some fix their eyes on the next goal, hoping that more achievement will bring the fulfillment they have longed for and so desperately need. This is simply a trap in the success cycle that leaves one exhausted, burnt out, and ready to give up.

What you do does matter. There is nothing wrong with finding success in your business. The problem is that all too often, success has become the ultimate goal of worth. However, God gives us an alternative. Pivot towards living a life of significance that will bring joy and meaning that success alone could never accomplish.

In the opening chapter of Philippians, Paul underscores the call to lead humble lives, prioritizing serving others above serving ourselves. By doing so, we mirror the heart of Jesus, adopting a servant's perspective rather than exploiting situations for personal success.

Through Christ's example, we are compelled to impact others, driven by the profound impact Jesus had on us when he prioritized our well-being over his own. In our business endeavors, we throw off selfish ambition; instead, every encounter becomes an opportunity for transformation, transcending mere financial transactions.

Just because someone finds success in this business does not automatically mean they are making contributions of significance into the lives of others. However, someone who pursues significance will always find success.

All the success we can experience in one lifetime, if not tied to making a significant impact in the lives of others, will never help us walk in the fulfillment God has set aside for us. Moving forward, may we see success through the lens of Christ, knowing that actual achievement comes from significantly impacting the lives God has set before us to encounter.

66 —
We have a drive to impact others because we have been greatly impacted by Jesus.

MATTHEW 6:21

FOR WHERE
YOUR TREASURE
IS, THERE YOUR
HEART WILL BE
ALSO.

20

KINDNESS

*"Put on then, as God's chosen ones, holy and beloved, compassionate hearts,
kindness, humility, meekness, and patience, bearing with one another and,
if one has a complaint against another, forgiving each other; as the Lord
has forgiven you, so you also must forgive. And above all these put on love,
which binds everything together in perfect harmony."*
Colossians 3:12-14 ESV

few years back, we had a God-ordained conversation that
lit a fire in our hearts to lead differently. One of the greatest
leaders we've had the privilege of knowing is an executive with
the social selling company we partner with. Every interaction we
ever have leaves us better as he leads with integrity, character,
and a genuine love for others. In the midst of our interaction
with him, the topic naturally turned towards discussing
leadership.

We posed a question: "Was there one leadership quality he
deemed most crucial in business?" His immediate response,
though unexpected, continues to resonate with us to this very
day. Without a moment's hesitation, he asserted, "kindness."

According to him, kindness is the most underrated yet
crucially needed tool for any leader. He explained that
developing kindness is challenging without having experienced
it firsthand. Kindness, he noted, serves as an overarching
leadership trait, encompassing humility, patience, forgiveness,
and compassion. It influences as well as nurtures these other
qualities.

Kindness never gets old, and you can never get enough of it. Kind leaders do not serve out of obligation but out of a response from previously encountering such kindness. Genuine kindness is a reflection of the love shown to us by Jesus. As Christ displays, serving others does not come with strings attached or selfish gains to be had.

The passage above in Colossians states we must put on "compassion, kindness, humility, and meekness." It also states that we are to "bear with one another" through conflict and forgive completely, just like we have been forgiven in Christ. No matter how "good" of a person we think we are, there is no way to cultivate such a mentality of kindness and forgiveness apart from Christ.

The Social Selling industry is rightly referred to as the "people business," and it's almost impossible to succeed in this industry if you do not desire to work with others. People are our passion, but people can be messy.

Since we are all flawed humans, there will be times in your business when you must forgive and ask for forgiveness. Sometimes, you will want to "put on" anger, resentment, or frustration; however, that does not serve you or the mission Jesus has given you.

Within your business, ask God if there is bitterness or unforgiveness that needs to be released. As resentment is released, God will unveil a new level of leadership.

We find harmony in our lives through Christ, who allows us to "put on" our new self that has been redeemed. This transformation will enable us to show up meek, patient, compassionate, and kind.

We are prepared to forgive, we are ready to create a culture of kindness, and we are in harmony with our team and our purpose. Any act of kindness that reflects the very heart of God is never wasted and is always felt by others.

66 ——

Genuine kindness is a reflection of the kindness shown to us by Jesus.

PROVERBS
21:21

WHOEVER PURSUES
RIGHTEOUSNESS
AND KINDNESS
WILL FIND LIFE,
RIGHTEOUSNESS,
AND HONOR.

21

HOLY ACTIVITY

"And the Lord will guide you continually and satisfy your desire in scorched places and make your bones strong; and you shall be like a watered garden, like a spring of water, whose waters do not fail. And your ancient ruins shall be rebuilt; you shall raise up the foundations of many generations; you shall be called the repairer of the breach, the restorer of streets to dwell in."
Isaiah 58:11-12 ESV

Holy action requires holy intentions. When Christ guides our intentions, our actions become a reflection of His goodness. It's a remarkable opportunity to infuse holiness into our entrepreneurship. In this industry, God has bestowed upon us the privilege of demonstrating that we not only seek blessings but also aspire to bless others through our endeavors.

The historical backdrop for the passage above in Isaiah 58 is that the people of Israel are fasting, asking God for deliverance, following their exile to Babylon. Zechariah 7:3-5 indicates that Israel fasted the fifth and seventh months for seventy years following the destruction of Jerusalem.

The people are desperately seeking justice from the Lord but fear that God has not heard their cries or seen their holy activity of fasting. Their frustration is palpable in this passage as they exhibit an expectant attitude. They anticipate that God should reciprocate with deliverance in response to their remarkable acts of spirituality. We see this in Isaiah 58:2 when they lament, "Why have we fasted, and you see it not?"

The people complain that God has turned His back on them and withheld justice. The Lord responds by asking Israel to stop depriving those around them of justice and righteousness. Even though Israel has been adhering to the Law and even participates in fasting, they have entirely neglected to let God's law impact their activity.

Although they believe they are seeking God through their fasts, they forget that Isaiah had earlier instructed that they were to "seek justice, rescue the oppressed, defend the orphan, plead for the widow" (Isaiah 1:17). However, Israel at this time is willing to participate in fasting as their worship of God, but not ready to take action that is pleasing to Him and informed by His commands.

Despite Israel missing the connection between holy action and intent, the Lord is merciful by telling them in Isaiah 58:10 that if they "pour themselves out for the hungry and satisfy the desire of the afflicted, then shall your light rise in the darkness and your gloom be as the noonday." God is connecting their holy acts with righteous motivations.

Putting God's commands into action will satisfy the scorched places in their hearts. They will be like an overflowing watered garden that brings life to others, and the areas in which they dwell will be forever changed (Isaiah 58:11-12). Their activity will reflect the nature of God, and their hearts will connected to His desires.

All of the business activities, all of the achievements, and all of the dreams mean little if they do not reflect the heart of God. It is only worth crying aloud to the Lord for guidance and favor if our intentions are centered on serving others and reflecting His glory.

Friend, your activity matters. It can change the trajectory of those who have very little margin in their lives. God will guide you, strengthen you, and bring fulfillment to the scorched places in your life as you serve others in this industry. You are so much more than an active entrepreneur in Social Selling. You are a repairer of the breach and restorer of the streets in which you dwell.

> **"**
> *You are a repairer of the breach and restorer of the streets in which you dwell.*

ISAIAH 58:10

IF YOU POUR YOURSELF OUT FOR THE HUNGRY AND SATISFY THE DESIRE OF THE AFFLICTED , THEN SHALL YOUR LIGHT RISE IN THE DARKNESS AND YOUR GLOOM BE AS THE NOONDAY.

HOLY TRUST

22

YOUR GOOD

"And we know that for those who love God all things work together
for good, for those who are called according to his purpose."
Romans 8:28 ESV

God is always seeking your good. Always. Trust that God has your best interests at heart both in the moments of struggle and victory. Trust involves not anticipating that God will provide everything you desire but believing that He will furnish everything you truly need.

Sometimes, God's seeming silence perplexes us, especially when we earnestly pray for answers. Other times, the answer is a closed door. Regardless of the answer, God sees the full picture and is working it out for His glory.

A notable example is when we stepped away from pastoral ministry. The church had experienced tremendous growth; we served alongside a team of godly leaders, and God was moving in mighty ways in so many lives. However, despite experiencing all this goodness, God stirred in our hearts that it was time to pass the baton on to another pastor.

It didn't make immediate sense, and honestly, it broke our hearts, but we trusted that God knew what was needed to work out the good for His glory. Trusting in God, in small or grand situations, is trust that is always well-founded.

Even in our struggle to trust at times, God does not stop crafting a future for our good and His good pleasure. We could never imagine that shifting out of pastoral ministry would lead to even more opportunities to shepherd others. We have witnessed people come to faith in Jesus after a team call, baptized new believers on a company trip, and seen miracle after miracle in the lives we get to engage with.

Romans 8:28 states that God is always "making all things work together for good" for those who love Him and are called to His purpose. What is this "good" Paul speaks of, and how can we define it? He tells us in Romans 8:1 when he proclaims, "There is no condemnation for those who are in Christ Jesus." That is the good God has worked out for us.

Even though we have fallen short of God's glory, we are not condemned because of who we become in Christ. Our ultimate good is salvation, and any other good that comes our way has been worked out by God because we are His.

Our definition of "good" may not align with God's, yet we can be confident that God's concept of good surpasses any imagination of ours. According to the verse, this promise is specifically for those purposefully called by the Lord. When we align with our purpose, trust in our calling, and allow the love of God to fill us, we can rest assured that our well-being unfolds before us.

Faith is trusting that we serve a good, good Father who cares about every detail of our life, working behind the scenes that ultimately leads to our good.

Trust is not always built on foreseeing what God has planned for us but on the certainty that whatever it is, it will be for our good and, more significantly, for His glory. Regardless of the season you find yourself in, be assured that a God who has redeemed and called you to His purpose is actively working it all out.

" ────

Trust is mot believing that God will give you all that want. It is believing that He will give you all that you need.

1 CORINTHIANS
2:9

BUT, AS IT IS WRITTEN,
"WHAT NO EYE HAS SEEN,
NOR EAR HEARD , NOR
THE HEART OF MAN
IMAGINED, WHAT GOD
HAS PREPARED FOR
THOSE WHO LOVES HIM.

23

SPIRITUAL INTELLIGENCE

"Blessed is the man who trusts in the Lord, whose trust is the Lord. He is like a tree planted by water, that sends out its roots by the stream, and does not fear when heat comes, for its leaves remain green, and is not anxious in the year of drought, for it does not cease to bear fruit."
Jeremiah 17: 7-8 ESV

The concept of "emotional intelligence" is one that is crucial when working with people. This idea simply means it is one's capacity to regulate and express emotion in an appropriate way. Rather than reacting to a stressful situation, a person with high emotional intelligence is inclined to respond thoughtfully, taking time to manage their own feelings and consider various perspectives. Developing a high level of emotional intelligence allows leaders to navigate the ups and downs of entrepreneurship, especially when in the people business.

While high emotional intelligence is vital in this journey, we've discovered that maintaining a deep spiritual intelligence is all the more important. The idea of spiritual intelligence surfaced as we observed many Christians in this industry quitting after encountering obstacles or falling short of goals.

Where belief was once unshakable, these setbacks can be an open door to the enemy creating doubt that this business is God's will. If ease or success becomes the sole criterion for discerning God's will, then perseverance in anything would be impossible.

Spiritual intelligence is trusting that just because we face opposition does not mean God is calling us away from a path we once so strongly believed we were supposed to be on. It's trusting that He called you to it and will sustain you, even on the hard days when overwhelm, doubt, and frustration hits.

It may be embarrassing to admit, but more than likely, most of us have used the "green light" miracle to gain confirmation on what the Lord wants us to do. You know, when you are driving somewhere, talking to God in your car, and convincing yourself that if you hit all the green lights on your way to your destination, that is a sign from God to move forward with a particular decision. Ok, maybe you have not done that exact thing, but more than likely, you have probably tried to decipher God's will through some random occurrences that you believe are God's way of showing you what to do.

The best thing about God's will is that it is not based on luck or chance. It is based on His perfect sovereignty. God's will for your life is also not controlled by your performance but by His power.

In His sovereign will, we find confidence that He guides us toward a space where our closeness to Him deepens and our reflection of Jesus intensifies. Embracing God's calling for our lives and placing our trust in Him is akin to the imagery in Jeremiah 17, where we, like a tree, plant our roots deeply, with the hopeful expectation of bearing fruit.

Grounded in God's promises, we send our roots out to seek refreshing waters so we may bear fruit. We do not worry about the heat that may come and try to make our leaves wither. We are not anxious about whether or not we will bear as much fruit as we expected. We do not fear seasons of drought because we know that, in the end, we will bear the fruit that the Lord wishes us to bring forth.

You may be just starting your business and feel completely overwhelmed with how to proceed. You may be a seasoned veteran but have experienced a time of drought. No matter your time within this industry, do not let your anxiety or a long winter season stop you from deepening your roots and seeking streams of refreshing waters.

Difficult situations in our business can strengthen our call if we face it with spiritual intelligence and renew our trust in God. May we face the seasons ahead with an assurance God will show us the way no matter what comes our way.

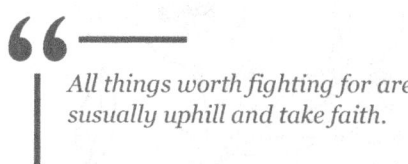

All things worth fighting for are susually uphill and take faith.

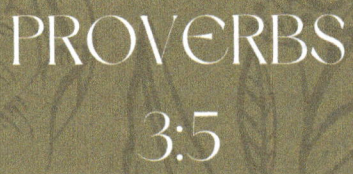

PROVERBS
3:5

TRUST IN THE LORD
WITH ALL YOUR
HEART, AND DO NOT
LEAN ON YOUR OWN
UNDERSTANDING.

24

SCARCITY

"When he saw the crowds, he had compassion for them, because they were harassed and helpless, like sheep without a shepherd. Then he said to his disciples, "The harvest is plentiful, but the laborers are few; therefore pray earnestly to the Lord of the harvest to send out laborers into his harvest."
Matthew 9:36-38 ESV

You matter. We want to emphasize this truth with unwavering conviction – you undeniably matter. Your efforts, your talents, your story all hold profound significance.

Sometimes, you may doubt your importance to God and the substantial contributions He has set aside for you. The enemy relentlessly strives to plant seeds of disbelief, attempting to persuade you that your presence lacks any meaningful impact on the world. This internal struggle epitomizes the battle we must wage against a scarcity mindset.

The scarcity mindset is a mental framework that individuals adopt when they perceive resources, opportunities, or success as limited, leading to a mindset of lack and fear of inadequacy. It is a belief system deeply rooted in the idea that God has ran out of use for us.

Dear friends, this life is not a zero-sum game where one person's victory equates to your loss. The Lord is abundant in grace, love, and opportunities. Your endeavors are not in vain, and you are not lagging behind in the tasks that God has entrusted to you.

Embracing an abundant mindset involves trusting that God has endless opportunities and resources for His children. Trusting that He is a good Father and holds nothing back.

In Matthew 9, we see that Jesus has compassion for a crowd that has been following Him and His disciples. Jesus had been performing miracles, yet He saw how much still needed to be done. Jesus addresses His disciples and makes a profound statement about the abundant opportunity for redemption surrounding them. However, He gravely points out that even though the "fields" are ripe for harvesting, there is a great need for more workers.

God has work for us, and it's not too late to pick up the plow, tend the fields, and await the harvest. We cannot let our human limitations convince us that we have no value and that there is nothing of value left to accomplish.

We serve a God of abundance — the owner of all we will ever see or experience. We are God's servants who have been tasked to work the fields and will gladly get our hands dirty to reap what was sowed.

The Lord of the harvest, the orchestrator of all, will never exhaust your opportunities to serve in His name. While the path may not be easy and requires great faith, the truth remains that there is an abundance of work to be done. He desires willing and moldable hearts that faithfully do the work needed.

Today, you might be grappling with the sense that your dreams no longer hold significance or that your prolonged pursuit has left you feeling unworthy due to limited progress. My dear friends, your dreams remain worth pursuing irrespective of a timeline because the Lord of the Harvest has planted them in your hearts.

You hold immense value in His grand plan, and He desires you to relish the joy of partnering with Him in your endeavors. Have faith that He comprehends the depths of your heart, understands your desires, and has a surplus of meaningful work destined for you. The harvest is ripe, awaiting its gathering, yet only some willing laborers exist. So, take hold of the plow, for there is an abundance that the Lord has intricately prepared for you.

66 ——

Your dreams are worth pursuing because the Lord of the harvest has placed them in your heart.

PSALM
31:19

OH, HOW ABUNDANT IS
YOUR GOODNESS, WHICH
YOU HAVE STORED UP FOR
THOSE WHO FEAR YOU AND
WORKED FOR THOSE WHO
TAKE REFUGE IN YOU, IN
THE SIGHT OF THE
CHILDREN OF MANKIND!

25

HEART POSITION

"Keep your heart with all vigilance, for from it flow the springs of life."
Proverbs 4:23 ESV

Laird Hamilton is quoted saying, "Make sure your worst enemy is not living between your own two ears." We know the real battle is a spiritual battle, and the battlefield can often be played out in the mind. Our thoughts shape our actions, and our actions, in turn, determine our outcomes. Every decision we make, our approach to situations, and our perception of our abilities collectively influence every facet of our business.

Continuously protecting what goes into our mind, as well as guarding what we allow to go on inside our mind, is so important because the enemy has come to steal, kill, and destroy. Identifying the false beliefs we entertain and replacing them with Truth is an ongoing practice. However, we believe God that there is a battle happening in our hearts as well.

The heart's position is the source of our motivation and the drive behind our actions. Protect the heart at all costs. With a Biblical mindset and heart position, you will have a firm foundation set that no man can shake, and the enemy is unable to get a foothold. Guided by a biblically informed heart, our aspirations are consistently centered on the ways and frequency with which we can serve others.

For Social Sellers, a Biblical heart position is focused on servanthood, Christ being at the center of our goals, and acting in a manner that aligns with Scripture. Solomon in Proverbs 4:23 urges us to protect our hearts with vigilance, which means that we are to daily position our hearts towards Christ so that all we do flows from the source.

You have an opportunity to be life-giving, truth-telling, and love-distributing in your Social Sales platform. However, your mindset must be set on the things above, and your heart must be aligned in the correct position. May the heart be the wellspring where the love of Christ overflows and grace reigns.

The Bible has a lot to say about both the heart and mind. In Philippians 4:8, we are urged to focus on honorable, pure, and truthful things. Mindset does not just determine how we think or act but impacts the trust we have in God.

It is the very lens of how we see God. Again, protect what you allow IN your mind and what you allow to go ON in your mind. Be the gatekeeper and protect the precious commodity that God has created and redeemed.

Similar to the Pharisees from Scripture, recalling the Word of God from memory becomes a hollow exercise if our hearts are not aligned with Jesus. The mere recitation of words lacks genuine meaning. The heart must be changed. Protect the position of the heart. The motivations and desires will either reflect the Kingdom or the world.

There will be times when you are tempted to cut corners, tell half-truths, or find some advantage that may deviate from your moral compass. Friends, no amount of success is worth positioning your heart away from Christ and towards temporal achievement.

Your heart has been mended and redeemed by Jesus. That new heart will flow springs of life that your network desperately needs to drink from. May our minds continually be molded by Scripture and our hearts tended by the Spirit. For when your heart is positioned towards others, you will encounter the joy of the Lord that has been set aside just for you.

66 ——

No amount of success is worth positioning your heart away from Christ and towards temporal achievement.

EZEKIEL
36:26

AND I WILL GIVE YOU A
NEW HEART, AND A NEW
SPIRIT I WILL PUT
WITHIN YOU. AND I WILL
REMOVE THE HEART OF
STONE FROM YOUR
FLESH AND GIVE YOU A
HEART OF FLESH.

26

IN YOUR CORNER

"The Lord will fight for you, and you have only to be silent."
Exodus 14:14 ESV

Despite our finite humanity destined for eternity with an infinite God, our natural inclination for control persists even when we affirm the Lord's sovereignty in our lives. While we sing about God fighting our battles in church, there are moments when we try to grab the steering wheel and white knuckle the drive.

Desiring control over our lives does not diminish our commitment as followers of Christ; rather, it aligns with human nature's inclination for assurance. This desire for control intensifies, particularly in the face of challenging conditions, because we want to avoid discomfort at all costs.

Through Holy Unrest, we have explored how your Social Selling business can be a platform for marketplace ministry. That ministry comes with many unknowns, challenges, and obstacles that can leave us feeling out of control. What if that very feeling of lack of control is what God is using as a refining tool?

The Lord calls us to work diligently, promising He is entirely in control. Nothing passes through His hands except what He allows.

The people of Israel, who had been enslaved for years under Pharaoh, had barely tasted freedom when they were met with an obstacle of faith. Standing on the beach of the Red Sea and with Pharaoh's army in hot pursuit, they lamented to Moses that it would have been better to stay under the wrath of Pharaoh back in Egypt than to be in this dire situation.

Despite witnessing the signs and wonders of God through Moses, they still doubted God's deliverance. They just wanted to go back to slavery because it was easier than the unknown. God heard their cries and spoke through Moses that they were to be silent and still and let God fight on their behalf. Despite their doubts, God parted the Red Sea and delivered His people to safety.

God is fighting on your behalf. He does not tire, He does not exhaust, and He is always in control. The Lord goes before us, and we can be still in His presence, knowing that victory and deliverance are at hand.

Isaiah 43:11 states, "But they who wait for the Lord shall renew their strength; they shall mount up with wings like eagles; they shall run and not be weary; they shall walk and not faint." God hears your cries, understands your fear, and sympathizes with your worry.

We do not need to charge forward absent the covering from God. We wait on the Lord, who will renew our strength, unburden us of our weariness, and will not allow us to fall behind.

At the onset of this 30-day journey, we emphasized the concept of working "heartily" for the Lord (Colossians 3:23), urging us to exert our utmost efforts. This entails executing our responsibilities as business owners to the best of our abilities, all while keeping Jesus at the forefront of our motivations.

Accompanied by this "heartily" work ethic comes a realization that God is sovereign. He controls every situation, fights our battles, and works things out for our good. Even when we find ourselves at the bank of our Red Sea, terrified that this is the obstacle we can't overcome. God is in control, making a way through the waters so we can step on the solid ground that He has already prepared for us.

Take today to stop white-knuckling your life, release control, and be still. Even though we do not know what the next moment may bring, God has already orchestrated that moment. Show up with confidence in the unknown because God is fighting your battle.

> 66
>
> *Even though we do not know what the next moment may bring, we know that moment has been orchestrated by a God who is acting on our behalf.*

ISAIAH 40:31

BUT THEY WHO WAIT FOR THE LORD SHALL RENEW THEIR STRENGTH; THEY SHALL MOUNT UP WITH WINGS LIKE EAGLES; THEY SHALL RUN AND NOT BE WEARY; THEY SHALL WALK AND NOT FAINT.

27

JUST IN TIME

"For everything there is a season, and a time for every matter under heaven."
Ecclesiastes 3:1 ESV

*E*verything has a season. That one verse from Ecclesiastes 3:1 brings comfort that surpasses all understanding. There is a time and season for every matter. There is a season of harvesting, but there is also a season of planting, watering, and a season of weeding. Regardless of our season, we can trust that it is His perfect time for the work He has for us.

God does not let us toil away endlessly out of teaching us a lesson or because He is too busy helping someone else reap the harvest. Each season is intentional, valuable, and purpose-filled. Rest assured that you are not forgotten, and thank God that He is the Master Gardener over your life and business.

For a seed to take root and break forth into a harvest, it must first be planted deep down in the dark soil. The waiting is a vulnerable time, but a period of growth, trusting we will soon breakthrough the surface.

We want to hurry up and get out of this dirt, basking in the sun, blooming in our potential. Don't miss that the healthy harvest comes from toiling, the struggle of taking root and breaking through the ground. Your current season that God has you in is purposed for much growth.

Waiting is undeniably challenging yet profoundly transformative when orchestrated by the Lord's hand. Embracing God's perfect timing alters external circumstances and reshapes us internally. It fosters humility in acknowledging our lack of control, vulnerability in admitting we cannot dictate our timeline, and cultivates patience.

While we eagerly anticipate what we want and need, our responsibility lies in faithfully navigating the specific season. The duration of our season may remain uncertain, but one thing that is certain is that waiting is a universal experience.

We tend to celebrate only the mountaintop victories, but the valley is where the fruit grows. The journey of an entrepreneur is simply going from valley to valley, with a quick stop on each mountaintop to reflect on what you've accomplished and where you are going.

The valley is not something to fear but rather a place where the fruit is forged. This is where profound personal growth transpires, and you become the leader needed for the next climb.

Ecclesiastes 3:1 beautifully encapsulates this truth, proclaiming there is a time for everything. Whether your time is to be planted, grow, or bloom, God sees and knows your place in your current season.

Friend, your season is not wasted. Not in the slightest bit.

Though we desire to know when God's timing will come to fruition, we can be assured that there is no other perfect timeline we would rather be in than His. God is not wasting your waiting, and there is power in your patience. With expectant hearts, may we wait on the Lord as He brings forth the fruit of our labor.

God is always working in our waiting with love and wisdom.

LAMENTATIONS
3:25

THE LORD IS GOOD
TO THOSE WHO
WAIT FOR HIM, TO
THE SOUL WHO
SEEKS HIM.

28

I SURRENDER

*"Humble yourselves, therefore, under the mighty hand of God so
that at the proper time he may exalt you, casting all your
anxieties on him, because he cares for you."*

1st Peter 5:6-7 ESV

The word "surrender" usually has a negative connotation associated with it. It often evokes a sense of loss, defeat, and weakness. No one wants to be on the side that surrenders in a battle or competition. However, when it comes to our Heavenly Father, surrender can be one of the most transformative freedoms one can experience. A holy trust where we can give everything to God because we know in Him is safety.

In 2006, we lived in a small college town in Illinois, far from family or familiarity. With a recent Master's degree in Political Science in hand as we welcomed our firstborn child into our family, we had grand plans of pursuing a Ph.D. and teaching at the university level.

While we had our life all planned out for the next several years, there was something missing... peace. While we had everything we had hoped for and were carving out a stable career, there was a deep nudge in our hearts that our perfectly planned life was no longer a blueprint we needed to build. It didn't seem very intelligent to even entertain that thought after spending years (and a lot of money) in graduate school.

One evening, while rocking our newborn son to sleep, we felt overwhelmed by God's presence. A word kept coming to mind again and again. "Surrender."

We struggled for months to know what exactly that "surrender" was meant for, but we knew we had to lay down our plans. With complete peace in our hearts, we moved back home to Texas and waited for the Lord to show us our next steps. It was one of those seasons of life that did not make sense from the outside perspective, but inward, we knew we were walking by faith.

Driving back from church one day, out of nowhere, the call to "surrender" finally came into clear view. Seemingly out of nowhere, it came out of my mouth, "I think we are supposed to go into ministry." Surrender. Giving all of our plans to the Lord. Surrendering our lives to vocational ministry. Peace like we have never known before washed over us.

From that pivotal moment onward, we embarked on a fifteen-year journey filled with one adventure after another, witnessing the miraculous hand of God at work in the church as a pastoral family. Our decision to release our preconceived notions of what we should do and wholeheartedly surrender to what God called us to do set the stage for this incredible odyssey. While the path of surrender to ministry wasn't always easy, it undeniably constituted the precise season required to bring us to where we find ourselves today.

God has a mission for us to partner with Him on but often we are too busy holding fast to our agenda. It is no wonder we live in a constant state of overwhelm and anxiety.

As Peter notes in 1 Peter 5:6-7, it is humbling to surrender to the Lord, but when we do, we can cast our anxieties about the future upon Him, knowing He truly cares about us.

Surrender over your worry, anxiety, and fear. He cares for you. He loves you. In our surrender, our trust in Him is well-founded as we wave the white flag of control and relinquish the battle to the Lord.

"———

God has a mission for us to partner with Him on but often we are too busy holding fast to our agenda. It is no wonder we live in a constant state of overwhelm and anxiety.

MATTHEW
11:29

TAKE MY YOKE UPON
YOU, AND LEARN FROM
ME, FOR I AM GENTLE
AND LOWLY IN HEART,
AND YOU WILL FIND
REST FOR YOUR SOULS.

THE OTHER SIDE

29

THE OTHER SIDE

"One day he got into a boat with his disciples, and he said to them, "Let us go across to the other side of the lake." So they set out, and as they sailed he fell asleep. And a windstorm came down on the lake, and they were filling with water and were in danger. And they went and woke him, saying, "Master, Master, we are perishing!" And he awoke and rebuked the wind and the raging waves, and they ceased, and there was a calm. He said to them, "Where is your faith?" And they were afraid, and they marveled, saying to one another, "Who then is this, that he commands even winds and water, and they obey him?"
Luke 8:22-25 ESV

Since living in the Pacific Northwest, the outdoor wonderland, a love for spending all our free time on the lake has taken root. Nestled in the mountains, the waters are so clear you can see every detail below the surface, and there is a stillness on the lake that brings peace to your soul.

Yet, during our latest excursion to the lake, tranquility was disrupted by an unexpected storm. We observed ominous clouds on the horizon, poised to ruin our day on the boat. The clouds eventually enveloped us, and a summer thunderstorm forced us to abandon the lake for a few hours.

Your entrepreneurship journey can mirror a tranquil lake, where the waters are serene, the surroundings peaceful, and the outlook promising. However, it is inevitable that storms blow in. It could be a customer canceling their account, a leader quitting, or falling short of your goal. Storms can be anticipated or arrive unexpectedly.

In Luke 8, Jesus imparts invaluable lessons on weathering storms. After a day of teaching and miracles, Jesus instructs His disciples in verse 22 to embark on a journey to the other side of the lake. He heads to the hull of the ship and quickly falls asleep.

As they set sail, a formidable storm descended upon the lake. The disciples, experienced fishermen familiar with the Sea of Galilee's waters, found themselves in a perilous situation as the boat filled with water. They immediately go and wake Jesus, crying out, "Master, Master, we are perishing!"

It's worth noting that even when they feel hopeless and fear for their lives, they still address Jesus as "Master." Though their fear was evident, many of the disciples probably assumed this would be their last boat ride; they still referred to Jesus as Master. It is also interesting that they did not attempt to maneuver out of the storm but instead turned to Jesus for deliverance. Even in the midst of perilous storms, we should still turn to the One who rests at the hull of our lives, helping us find a way through the storms.

Encountering various challenges like windstorms, white squalls, or typhoons throughout our business journey will come at the most unexpected times. Thankfully, we have our Master in the boat with us.

The disciples, confronted with a storm they couldn't handle, urgently turn to Jesus for assistance. Though their faith was shaken, their hearts new the only had one hope to get through this storm.

Jesus awakened rebukes the wind and raging waves, bringing about a calm. The disciples watched in awe of His authority over the winds and water.

While the immediate lesson is that Jesus has the power to calm our storms, it's important to note that not every storm is instantly pacified. We sometimes navigate through turbulent seas, shaken and battered, before the storms subside. Yet, each storm endured with Jesus at the helm instills confidence that He will never abandon us, regardless of the storm's intensity.

Particular storms in our lives may persist until we reach the other side of heaven. Not every storm is meant to come to an end during our lifetime. Though we may not live to experience the full peace of calm waters, Jesus' control over them is not diminished.

If you look back at the beginning of this passage, Jesus tells His disciples, "Let's go to the other side." Jesus knew that the storm was not going to take them out. Christ made a promise to His disciples that they were going to get to the other side.

Jesus knew the storm was coming and rested in the ship's hull because He also knew they would safely land on the other side, even if they had to sail through a storm first.

Christ has placed goals, dreams, and a vision for the greater good and God's glory within your heart. When your business encounters storms, the Master of the wind and waves won't let you veer off course. He remains steadfast no matter how much the boat rocks.

The other side, for Social Sellers following Christ, isn't defined by ranks, titles, or paychecks. The other side is a deeper relationship with Him, an enhanced comprehension of God's provision, love, grace, and mission. It represents a ministry within an industry capable of impacting countless lives.

The most formidable storm we've faced isn't rooted in our roles as Social Sellers; it's the separation from God due to our sins. Jesus entered that storm, guiding us to the serene waters of God's grace. If Jesus can bring peace to the chaos of that profound existential storm, there is no storm in our business or life that is beyond His ability to navigate.

66 ——

Even when the wind and waves seem like they will overtake you, the Lord of the storms will not let you perish.

A HOLY FUTURE

30

A HOLY FUTURE

"For I know the plans I have for you, declares the Lord, plans for welfare and not for evil, to give you a future and a hope."
Jeremiah 29:11 ESV

For the last 30 days, you have uncovered what it means to have a "holy unrest" within your Social Selling business. Complete fulfillment with Christ and simultaneously passionate to pursue a greater impact that will make much of Jesus to the world around us. We can approach our entrepreneurship with the holy unrest that drives our business forward in a manner that honors Christ and increases a platform for the gospel.

Our identity is secure in Jesus within the holy unrest stirring, no matter our accomplishments or failures along the way. There is a calling on each of our lives that aligns our motives with God's mission. Our actions can be holy within this industry and not reflect the world's ways. Finally, our trust is well founded in the Lord as we navigate our faith and business.

The future is secure, even if it is unknown. We serve the God who oversees our tomorrow and can confidently face each day with expectant hearts that the miraculous is right around the corner. As we hope you have realized throughout the past 30 days, it is by no accident you are in this industry and God has so much He still means to accomplish through your holy unrest.

The Social Selling industry will continue to evolve and grow. New methods will be developed, and new leaders will emerge. However, the truth of God's Word and our security in Jesus will never change.

If you were to poll believers on one of the most well-known verses in Jeremiah, almost assuredly, Jeremiah 29:11 would be at the top. Commonly found on bumper stickers, signs, and coffee cups to encourage people that God will work out everything in their lives, we believe Jeremiah speaks on something much more significant than our future prosperity.

Jeremiah 29:11 states, "For I know the plans I have for you, declares the Lord, plans for welfare and not for evil, to give you a future and a hope." In this context, Jeremiah addresses the captive people of Judah under Babylonian rule, assuring them of their impending deliverance rather than promising future earthly wealth.

As Christian Social Sellers, we often gravitate toward these verses, desiring a bright future for our business. We consistently seek God's blessings on our endeavors, aspiring to be a blessing to others and our families.

However, it's crucial to understand that the plans the Lord has executed on your behalf and His future plans for you aren't primarily about amassing earthly success but rather experiencing an abundant life in Jesus.

We can work diligently towards our goals in business because we are no longer desperate to find our fulfillment in the achievement. We do not fear that future opportunities will be scarce, but we cling to our security with the Lord that His plans for us have hope that knows no bounds.

A holy future awaits you that will reflect the nature of God, the peace that the gospel provides, and the grace we are washed with. The Lord of your tomorrow has placed you in the Social Selling industry with specific gifts, connected to a community, and a dream in your heart for a time such as this.

As brothers and sisters in Christ, we maintain an identity that begins and ends with Jesus —adhering to a clear calling that resounds in our hearts.

With a holy unrest, we live out our purpose in this beautiful industry, passionate about using our platform for the good of others and the glory of God. May the Lord's presence accompany you as you continue this journey, magnifying His name and tirelessly proclaiming His holy message of redemption.

> *We serve the God who oversees our tomorrow and can confidently face each day with expectant hearts that the miraculous is right around the corner.*

Contact Us

🌐 theraneyco.com

✉ hello@theraneyco.com

Anthem.Network

🌐 theraneyco.com/anthem

ⓕ anthem.network

ⓘ @anthem.network

Our Social

ⓘ @them.raneys

▷ @them.raneys

ⓕ facebook.com/theraneyco

Made in the USA
Monee, IL
12 December 2023

48982561R00079